MIGHTY MACHINES IN ACTION

Bulldozers

by Chris Bowman

BLASTOFF! READERS 2

BELLWETHER MEDIA • MINNEAPOLIS, MN

Note to Librarians, Teachers, and Parents:

Blastoff! Readers are carefully developed by literacy experts and combine standards-based content with developmentally appropriate text.

Level 1 provides the most support through repetition of high-frequency words, light text, predictable sentence patterns, and strong visual support.

Level 2 offers early readers a bit more challenge through varied simple sentences, increased text load, and less repetition of high-frequency words.

Level 3 advances early-fluent readers toward fluency through increased text and concept load, less reliance on visuals, longer sentences, and more literary language.

Level 4 builds reading stamina by providing more text per page, increased use of punctuation, greater variation in sentence patterns, and increasingly challenging vocabulary.

Level 5 encourages children to move from "learning to read" to "reading to learn" by providing even more text, varied writing styles, and less familiar topics.

Whichever book is right for your reader, Blastoff! Readers are the perfect books to build confidence and encourage a love of reading that will last a lifetime!

This edition first published in 2017 by Bellwether Media, Inc.

No part of this publication may be reproduced in whole or in part without written permission of the publisher. For information regarding permission, write to Bellwether Media, Inc., Attention: Permissions Department, 5357 Penn Avenue South, Minneapolis, MN 55419.

Library of Congress Cataloging-in-Publication Data

Names: Bowman, Chris, author.
Title: Bulldozers / by Chris Bowman.
Description: Minneapolis, MN : Bellwether Media, Inc., [2017] | Series:
    Blastoff! Readers. Mighty Machines in Action | Audience: Ages 5-8. |
    Audience: K to grade 3. | Includes bibliographical references and index.
Identifiers: LCCN 2016032048 (print) | LCCN 2016033098 (ebook) | ISBN
    9781626176010 (hardcover : alk. paper) | ISBN 9781681033310 (ebook)
Subjects: LCSH: Bulldozers–Juvenile literature.
Classification: LCC TA725 .B63 2017 (print) | LCC TA725 (ebook) | DDC
    629.225–dc23
LC record available at https://lccn.loc.gov/2016032048

Editor: Christina Leighton   Designer: Jon Eppard

Printed in the United States of America, North Mankato, MN.

Table of Contents

A bulldozer crawls up to a **construction site**. It is there to make the ground even.

First, it uses its **ripper** to tear through the rocks.

ripper

5

Then the dozer pushes the rocks and dirt with its **blade**.

blade

Soon, the area is clear. Building can begin!

Bulldozers are powerful machines that push, dig, and lift.

They often work in construction. They move rocks, dirt, and other heavy objects.

MACHINE PROFILE
CATERPILLAR D9T

length: 27 feet (8.2 meters)
height: 13 feet (4 meters)
power: 436 horsepower (325 kilowatts)

Bulldozers also work in **mines** and on roads.

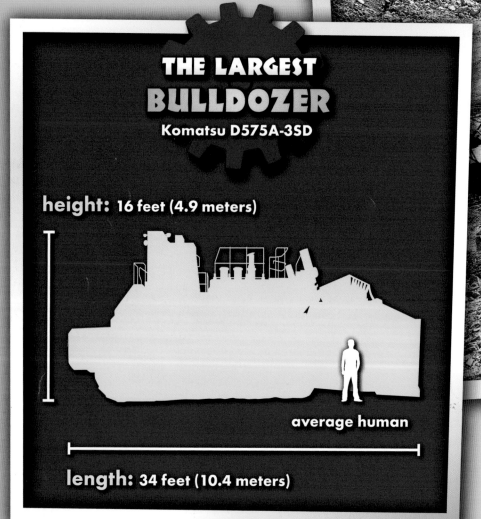

THE LARGEST
BULLDOZER
Komatsu D575A-3SD

height: 16 feet (4.9 meters)

average human

length: 34 feet (10.4 meters)

They clear bushes and trees.
They also dig ditches.

BLADES, RIPPERS, AND TRACKS

All bulldozers have blades on the front. **Straight blades** are short. They **level** the ground.

straight
blade

universal blade

Universal blades are tall and curved. They are used for carrying and digging.

Many dozers also have rippers. These look like big claws. They dig into the ground.

The bulldozers pull the rippers behind them. This breaks up rocks and hard ground.

Most bulldozers have **tracks**. The tracks are wide and move in a loop.

tracks

They help the machines move
on uneven ground.

Some dozers have wheels instead. They move more quickly and easily.

These dozers usually perform lighter tasks on hard ground.

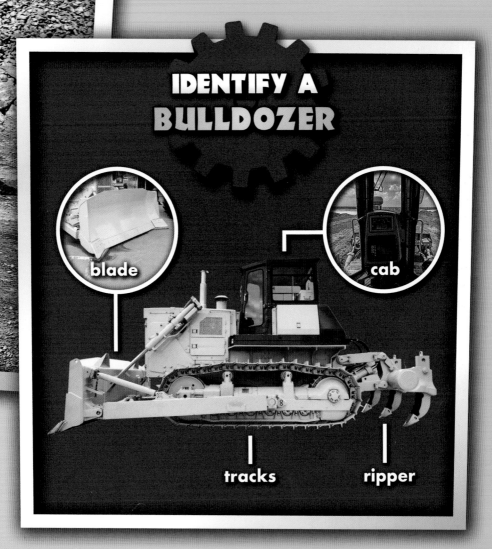

IDENTIFY A BULLDOZER

blade

cab

tracks

ripper

NOISY MOVERS

Bulldozers have big **diesel engines**. These make loud noises as they work.

Bulldozers need the power to
do all types of jobs!

Glossary

blade—a large metal plate that works like a shovel

construction site—a place where something is built

diesel engines—loud engines that burn diesel fuel and are often used in big machines

level—to make flat and even

mines—pits or tunnels from which materials are collected

ripper—a sharp tool used to break apart rocks and hard ground

straight blades—short, flat blades used to make ground even

tracks—large belts that move in a loop around gears

universal blades—big, curved blades used for digging and carrying; universal blades are also called U-blades.

To Learn More

AT THE LIBRARY
Clay, Kathryn. *Bulldozers*. North Mankato, Minn.:
Capstone Press, 2017.

Hayes, Amy. *Big Bulldozers*. New York, N.Y.:
Cavendish Square Publishing, 2016.

Lennie, Charles. *Bulldozers*. Minneapolis, Minn.:
Abdo Kids, 2015.

ON THE WEB
Learning more about bulldozers
is as easy as 1, 2, 3.

1. Go to www.factsurfer.com.

2. Enter "bulldozers" into the search box.

3. Click the "Surf" button and you will see a
   list of related web sites.

With factsurfer.com, finding more
information is just a click away.

Index